WHY DO I FEEL SO BAD?

First published in 2007 by Five Areas.
This edition first published in 2012 by Darton, Longman and Todd Ltd
1 Spencer Court, 140–142 Wandsworth High Street, London SW18 4JJ.

ISBN 978-0-232-52928-9

A catalogue record for this book is available from the British Library.
Printed and bound in Great Britain by Halstan & Co Ltd, Amersham.

Although we hope you find this book helpful, it's not intended to be a direct
substitute for consultative advice with a healthcare professional, nor does the
author or the publisher give any assurances about its effectiveness in a
particular case. Accordingly, neither the author nor the publisher shall be held
liable for any loss or damages arising from its use.

WHY DO I FEEL SO BAD?

Dr Chris Williams

DARTON · LONGMAN + TODD

Too Much to do
FRIENDS HATE ME
SOMEONE CLOSE IS REALLY ILL
LOST MY JOB
Got Dumped
BEING ILL
I'M ALL ALONE
Got kicked off the team
GOT CRITICISED
FAILED TEST OR EXAM
BEING BULLIED
No-one to talk to

You feel bad because you're in a vicious circle

The way you feel is affected by things that happen to you. Like the bad things on the opposite page. Those things are all outside of you. Sometimes, you can change what's happening outside, but often, you can't do much about them.

And when you allow them to affect your mood, the vicious circle kicks in and you feel worse and worse and worse...

Turn over to see how it works

Too much to do
FRIENDS HATE ME
SOMEONE CLOSE IS REALLY ILL
LOST MY JOB
Got Dumped
BEING ILL
ALTERED THINKING
I'M USELESS
I'M ALL ALONE
Got kicked off the team
GOT CRITICISED
FAILED TEST OR EXAM
BEING BULLIED
No-one to talk to

First, an outside event affects you

When something happens, you naturally notice it and think about it. If you forget your sister's birthday, for example, you may think 'I'm useless!' This is called **Altered Thinking.**

Altered thinking can set off a chain reaction inside you that affects the way you feel and what you do.

When your altered thinking is negative (like 'I'm useless'), the vicious circle is triggered and you can end up really down, not getting out of bed and even feeling ill. Let's watch the vicious circle in action.

Let's watch the
Vicious Circle in action

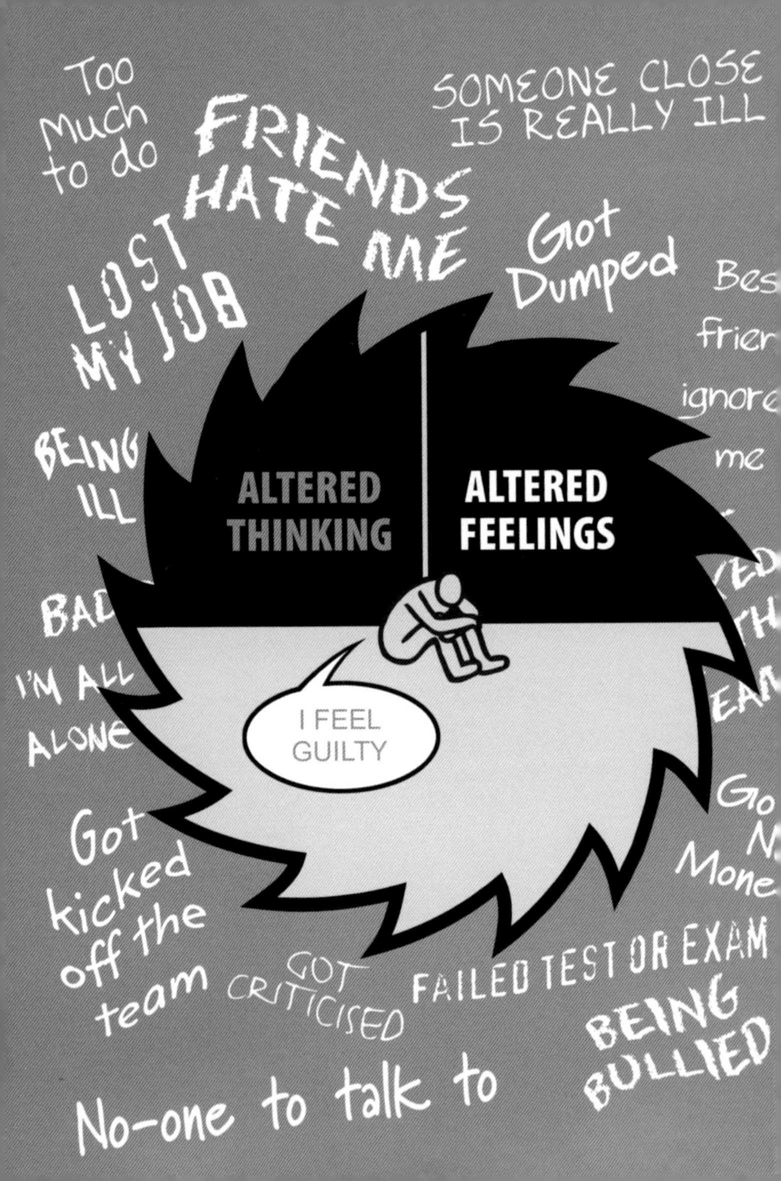

Too much to do
FRIENDS HATE ME
SOMEONE CLOSE IS REALLY ILL
LOST MY JOB
Got Dumped
BEING ILL
ALTERED THINKING
ALTERED FEELINGS
I'M ALL ALONE
I FEEL GUILTY
Got kicked off the team
GOT CRITICISED
FAILED TEST OR EXAM
BEING BULLIED
No-one to talk to

Altered thinking leads to altered feelings

If you think 'I'm useless!' you're going to feel pretty low, sad or guilty.

Maybe you feel as if you've let her down, or you might feel guilty because you know you should have been more organised.

So now
what happens?

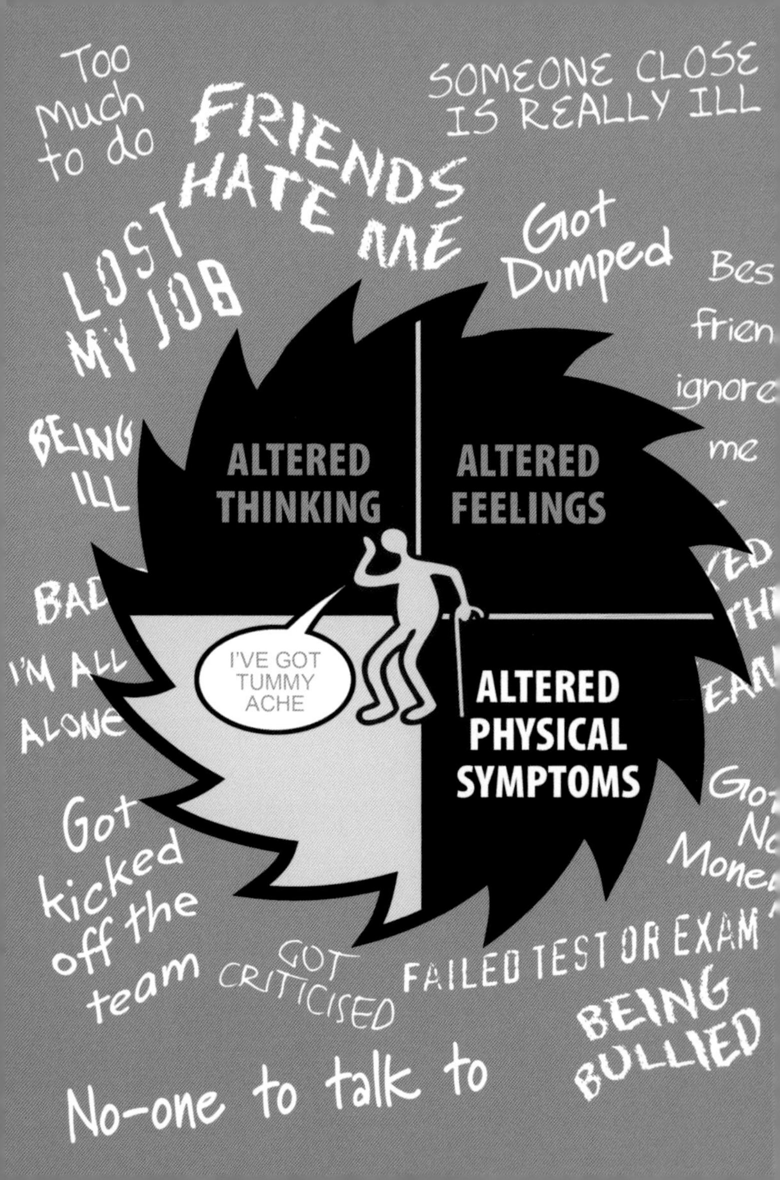

Altered feelings lead to altered physical symptoms

When you feel low or guilty,
you can get sweaty, tense with
stomach ache or headaches.
Sometimes you can feel really tired.

Your hands might feel clammy, or you
get an attack of the jitters and can't sit
still.

Ever had a sinking feeling or felt your
heart racing? It's probably that old
vicious circle spinning round!

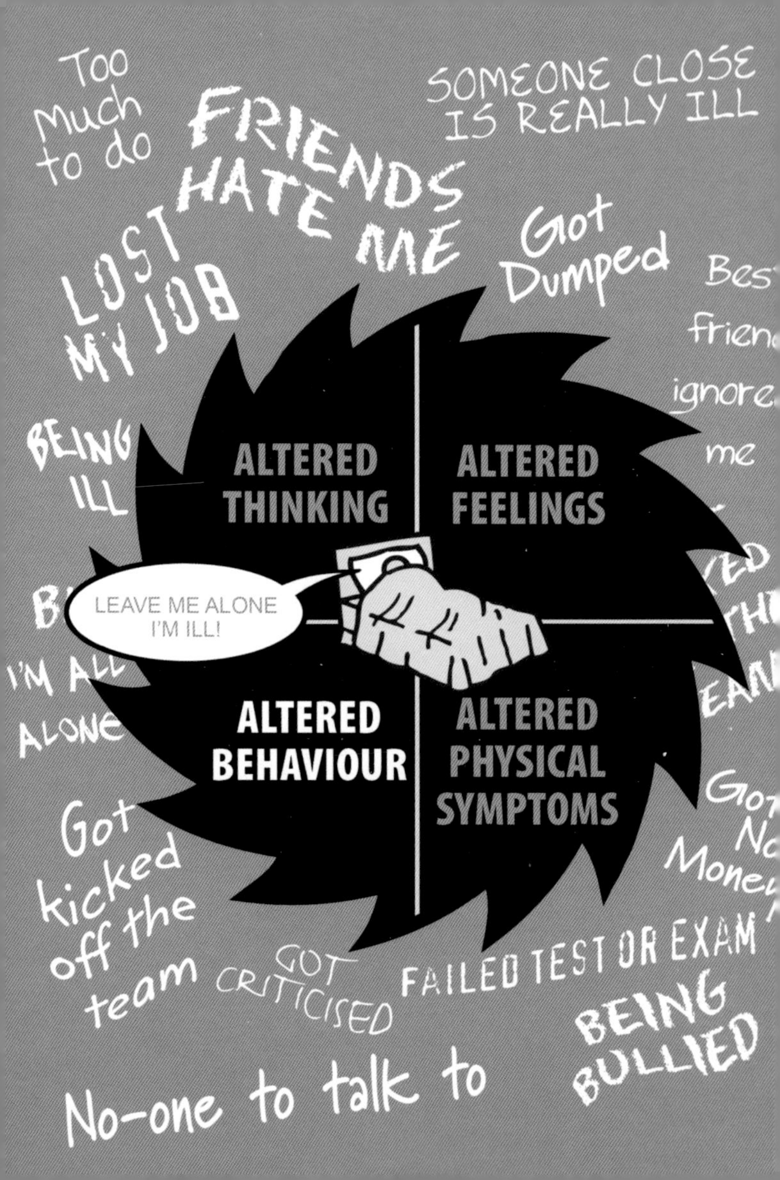

Altered physical symptoms lead to altered behaviour

It's only natural. You're really tired, you have a headache or maybe feel tense so you don't feel like going out, or even getting up. You steer clear of people who might ask if you sent a card or present. You stay in and hardly do any exercise. You're not eating right and you seem to catch all the bugs that are going round.

You might finish up at the doctor's, asking why you can't seem to shake off this virus you've had for weeks.

And you know what happens then? The circle goes round again, only this time, you're already ill, staying in bed and fed up, so you get even worse.

Now for the *good* news!

Vicious, these vicious circles, aren't they?

YOU CAN STOP THE CIRCLE!

You know the great thing about circles? They turn both ways!

In the same way that just one thing (an altered thought) led to everything else getting worse, you can start to make it better by changing one thing.

Just by eating differently or doing more exercise, or changing the way you think about some things, you can affect ALL THE OTHER THINGS IN THE CIRCLE and start to feel better.

Sounds too easy? Turn over for an example.

How to stop
the circle

2. This makes you feel bad – altered feelings

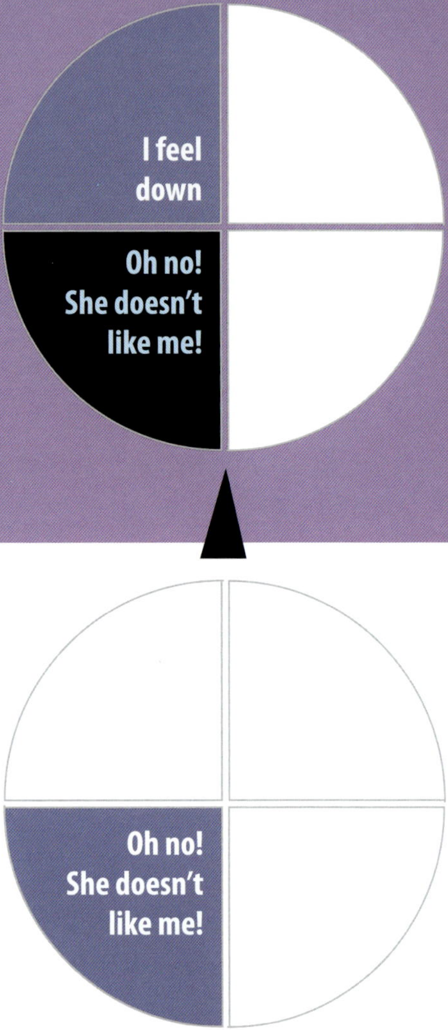
I feel down
Oh no! She doesn't like me!
Oh no! She doesn't like me!

1. You're walking down the street and someone you know ignores you.

start here

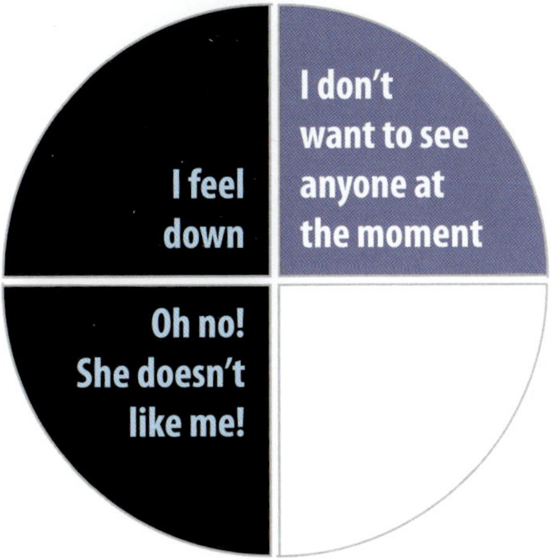
I feel down
I don't want to see anyone at the moment
Oh no! She doesn't like me!

3. You go home and avoid other people's company – altered behaviour

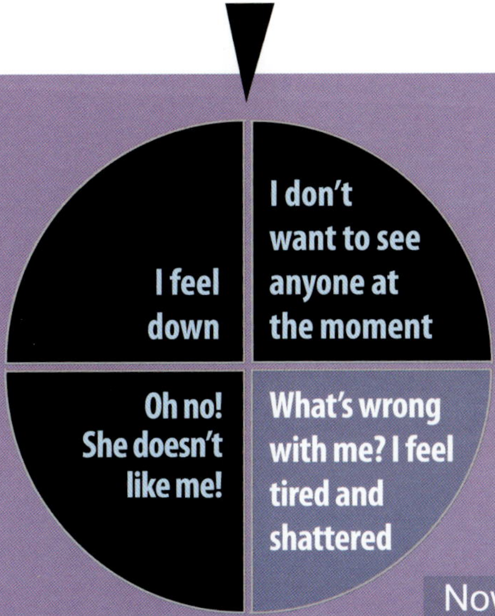
I feel down
I don't want to see anyone at the moment
Oh no! She doesn't like me!
What's wrong with me? I feel tired and shattered

4. You have no energy and maybe can't sleep that night for worrying about what happened – altered physical symptoms

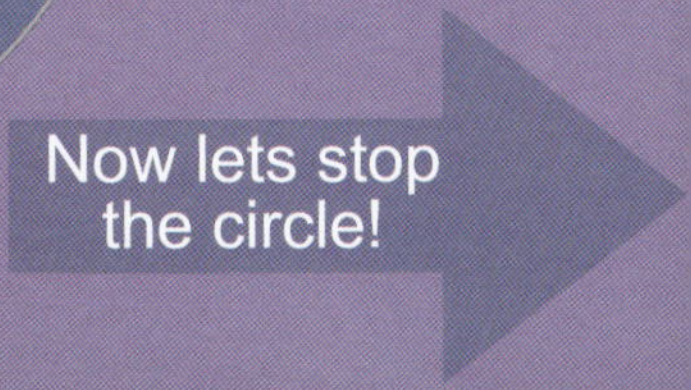
Now lets stop the circle!

2. You're concerned, so you run after her and ask her what's wrong

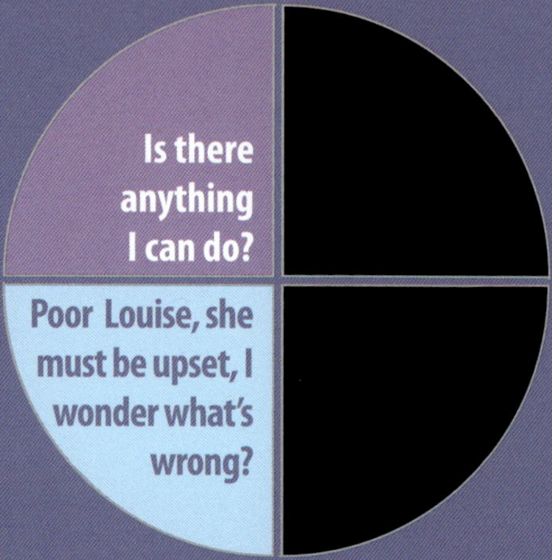
Is there anything I can do?
Poor Louise, she must be upset, I wonder what's wrong?

1. You're walking down the street and someone you know ignores you.

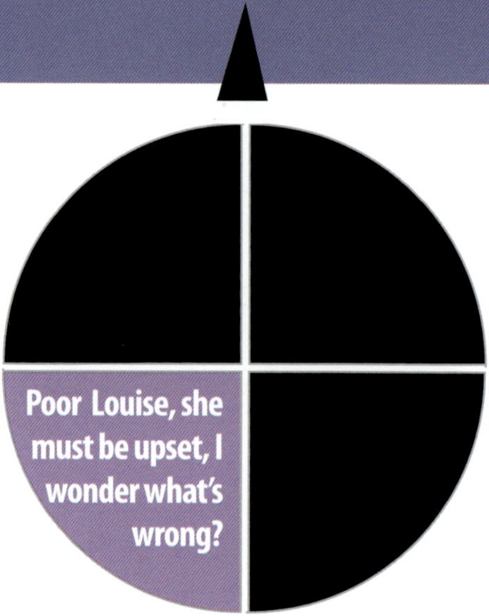
Poor Louise, she must be upset, I wonder what's wrong?

Start here

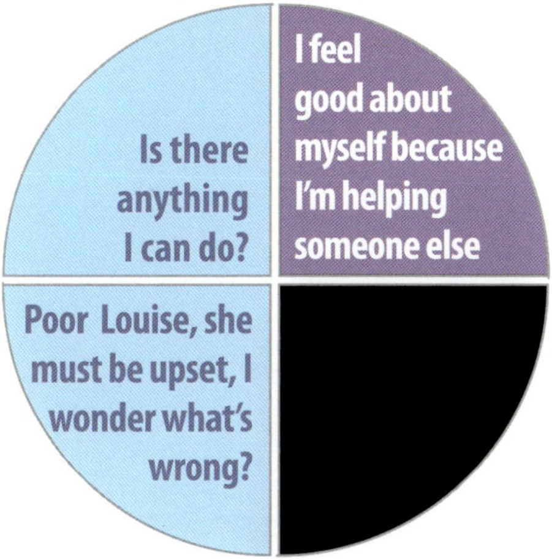
I feel good about myself because I'm helping someone else
Is there anything I can do?
Poor Louise, she must be upset, I wonder what's wrong?

3. Louise explains and you listen like a good friend

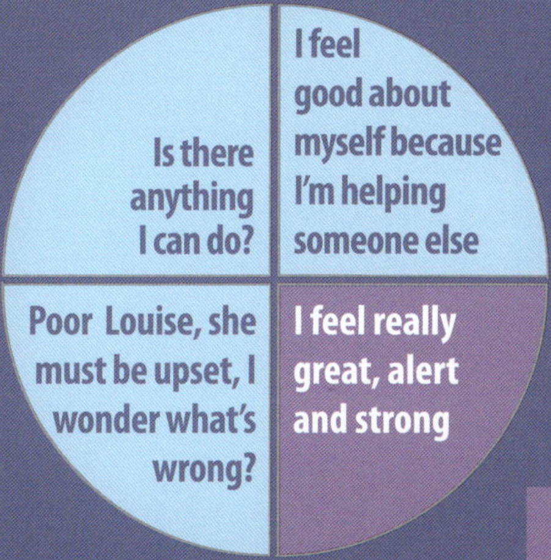
I feel good about myself because I'm helping someone else
Is there anything I can do?
Poor Louise, she must be upset, I wonder what's wrong?
I feel really great, alert and strong

4. You arrange to see Louise later and discuss practical things you can do to help

See how it works?

YOU HAVE CONTROL

You can take control and stop the vicious circle by changing just one thing – your thinking, your diet, your activities – almost anything. And it doesn't have to be a big thing!

You could start by changing the way you eat. By going out just one time. By doing just a bit more exercise. By changing the way you think about things.

If you manage to do something about just one thing, you'll break the vicious circle, stop it spinning down and down and start to feel better straight away.

Try it now!
Good Luck

ABOUT THIS BOOK

With websites receiving over 4 million hits a month and a wealth of supporting research data, the Five Areas Approach on which this book is based, devised by Dr Chris Williams, is one of the most widely-used CBT systems in the world.

Cognitive Behavioural Therapy (CBT) has a strong evidence base for helping people with low mood, anxiety and a growing range of other common mental and physical health difficulties.

Want to learn more about you? Turn things around in your life for the better? The Five Areas Approach can help you to do this. It takes the proven CBT model and makes it accessible and practical so that you can have the tools you need to help change things in your life – fast.

Please visit the Five Areas websites – www.llttf.com (free life skills course), www.llttfshop.com (bookshop) and www.fiveareasonline.com (online books) – to discover more about this work and see the other resources on offer.

Dr Chris Williams is Professor of Psychosocial Psychiatry at the University of Glasgow, UK, and is a past-President of the British Association for Behavioural and Cognitive Psychotherapies (www.babcp.com) – the lead body for CBT in the UK, Patron of the charities Anxiety UK and Triumph over Phobia and is a well-known CBT workshop leader and researcher.

PICK ME UP

Turn your life around – fast!

Available in the Pick Me Up range:

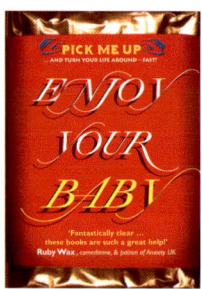

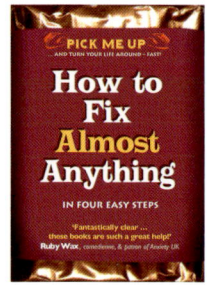

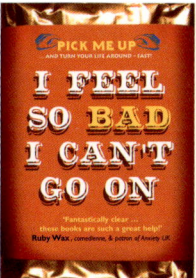